Biographical Stories

(From: "True Stories of History and Biography")

NATHANIEL HAWTHORNE

Biographical Stories
Nathaniel Hawthrone

© 1st World Library – Literary Society, 2004
PO Box 2211
Fairfield, IA 52556
www.1stworldlibrary.org
First Edition

LCCN: 2003099790

ISBN: 1-59540-112-1

Purchase *"Biographical Stories"*
as a traditional bound book at:
www.1stWorldLibrary.org/purchase.asp?ISBN=1-59540-112-1

1st World Library Literary Society is a nonprofit organization dedicated to promoting literacy by:

- Creating a free internet library accessible from any computer worldwide.
- Hosting writing competitions and offering book publishing scholarships.

Readers interested in supporting literacy through sponsorship, donations or membership please contact:
literacy@1stworldlibrary.org
Check us out at: www.1stworldlibrary.org

Biographical Stories
*contributed by Ed, Tim & Rodney
in support of
1st World Library Literary Society*

CONTENTS:

BENJAMIN WEST..........................15

SIR ISAAC NEWTON.....................28

SAMUEL JOHNSON......................44

OLIVER CROMWELL....................51

BENJAMIN FRANKLIN..................63

QUEEN CHRISTINA......................79

BIOGRAPHICAL STORIES

This small volume and others of a similar character, from the same hand, have not been composed without a deep sense of responsibility. The author regards children as sacred, and would not, for the world, cast anything into the fountain of a young heart that might imbitter and pollute its waters. And, even in point of the reputation to be aimed at, juvenile literature is as well worth cultivating as any other. The writer, if he succeed in pleasing his little readers, may hope to be remembered by them till their own old age, - a far longer period of literary existence than is generally attained by those who seek immortality from the judgments of full-grown men.

CHAPTER 1.

When Edward Temple was about eight or nine years old he was afflicted with a disorder of the eyes. It was so severe, and his sight was naturally so delicate, that the surgeon felt some apprehensions lest the boy should become totally blind. He therefore gave strict directions to keep him in a darkened chamber, with a bandage over his eyes. Not a ray of the blessed light of heaven could be suffered to visit the poor lad.

This was a sad thing for Edward. It was just the same as if there were to be no more sunshine, nor moonlight, nor glow of the cheerful fire, nor light of lamps. A night had begun which was to continue perhaps for months, - a longer and drearier night than that which voyagers are compelled to endure when their ship is icebound, throughout the winter, in the Arctic Ocean. His dear father and mother, his brother George, and the sweet face of little Emily Robinson must all vanish and leave him in utter darkness and solitude. Their voices and footsteps, it is true, would be heard around him; he would feel his mother's embrace and the kind pressure of all their hands; but still it would seem as if they were a thousand miles away.

And then his studies, - they were to be entirely given up. This was another grievous trial; for Edward's memory hardly went back to the period when he had not known how to read. Many and many a holiday had he spent at his hook, poring over its pages until the deepening twilight confused the print and made all the letters run into long words. Then, would he press his hands across his eyes and wonder why they pained him so; and when the candles were lighted, what was the reason that they burned so dimly, like the moon in a foggy night? Poor little fellow! So far as his eyes were concerned he was already an old man, and needed a pair of spectacles almost as much as his own grandfather did.

And now, alas! the time was come when even grandfather's spectacles could not have assisted Edward to read. After a few bitter tears, which only pained his eyes the more, the poor boy submitted to the surgeon's orders. His eyes were bandaged, and, with his mother on one side and his little friend Emily on the other, he was led into a darkened chamber.

"Mother, I shall be very miserable!" said Edward, sobbing.

"O no, my dear child!" replied his mother, elicerfully. "Your eyesight was a precious gift of Heaven, it is true; but you would do wrong to be miserable for its loss, even if there were no hope of regaining it. There are other enjoyments besides what come to us through our eyes."

"None that are worth having," said Edward.

"Ah, but you will not think so long," rejoined Mrs. Temple, with tenderness. "All of us - your father, and myself, and George, and our sweet Emily - will try to find occupation and amusement for you. We will use all our eyes to make you happy. Will they not be better than a single pair?"

"I will sit, by you all day long," said Emily, in her low, sweet voice, putting her hand into that of Edward.

"And so will I, Ned," said George, his elder brother, "school time and all, if my father will permit me."

Edward's brother George was three or four years older than himself, - a fine, hardy lad, of a bold and ardent temper. He was the leader of his comrades in all their enterprises and amusements. As to his proficiency at study there was not much to be said. He had sense and ability enough to have made himself a scholar, but found so many pleasanter things to do that he seldom took hold of a book with his whole heart. So fond was George of boisterous sports and exercises that it was really a great token of affection and sympathy when he offered to sit all day long in a dark chamber with his poor brother Edward.

As for little Emily Robinson, she was the daughter of one of Mr. Temple's dearest friends. Ever since her mother went to heaven (which was soon after Emily's birth) the little girl had dwelt in the household where we now find her. Mr. and Mrs. Temple seemed to love her as well as their own children; for they had no daughter except Emily; nor would the boys have known the blessing of a sister had not this gentle stranger come to teach them what it was. If I could show you Emily's face, with her dark hair smoothed away from her forehead, you would be pleased with her look of simplicity and loving kindness, but might think that she was somewhat too grave for a child of seven years old. But you would not love her the less for that.

So brother George and this loving little girl were to be Edward's companions and playmates while he should be kept prisoner in the dark chamber. When the first bitterness of his grief was over he began to feel that, there might be some comforts and enjoyments in life even for a boy whose eyes were covered with a bandage.

"I thank you, dear mother," said he, with only a few sobs; "and you, Emily; and you too, George. You will all be very kind to me, I know. And my father, - will not he come and see me every day?"

"Yes, my dear boy," said Mr. Temple; for, though invisible to Edward, he was standing close beside him. "I will spend some hours of every day with you. And as I have often amused you by relating stories and adventures while you had the use of your eyes, I can do the same now that you are unable to read. Will this please you, Edward?"

"O, very much," replied Edward.

"Well, then," said his father, "this evening we will begin the series of Biographical Stories which I promised you some time ago."

CHAPTER II.

When evening came, Mr. Temple found Edward considerably revived in spirits and disposed to be resigned to his misfortune. Indeed, the figure of the boy, as it was dimly seen by the firelight, reclining in a well-stuffed easy-chair, looked so very comfortable that many people might have envied hun. When a man's eyes have grown old with gazing at the ways of the world, it does not seem such a terrible misfortune to have them bandaged.

Little Emily Robinson sat by Edward's side with the air of an accomplished nurse. As well as the duskiness of the chamber would permit she watched all his motions and each varying expression of his face, and tried to anticipate her patient's wishes before his tongue could utter them. Yet it was noticeable that the child manifested an indescribable awe and disquietude whenever she fixed her eyes on the bandage; for, to her simple and affectionate heart, it seemed as if her dear friend Edward was separated from her because she could not see his eyes. A friend's eyes tell us many things which could never be spoken by the tongue.

George, likewise, looked awkward and confused, as stout and healthy boys are accustomed to do in the society of the sick or afflicted. Never having felt pain or sorrow, they are abashed, from not knowing how to sympathize with the sufferings of others.

"Well, my dear Edward," inquired Mrs. Temple, "is Your chair quite comfortable? and has your little nurse provided for all your wants? If so, your father is ready to begin his stories."

"O, I am very well now," answered Edward, with a faint smile. "And my ears have not forsaken me, though my eyes are good for nothing. So pray, dear father, begin."

It was Mr. Temple's design to tell the children a series of true stories, the incidents of which should be taken from the childhood and early life of eminent people. Thus he hoped to bring George, and Edward, and Emily into closer acquaintance with the famous persons who have lived in other times by showing that they also had been children once. Although Mr. Temple was scrupulous to relate nothing but what was founded on fact, yet he felt himself at liberty to clothe the incidents of his narrative in a new coloring, so that his auditors might understand them the better.

"My first story," said he, "shall be about a painter of pictures."

"Dear me!" cried Edward, with a sigh. "I am afraid I shall never look at pictures any more."

"We will hope for the best," answered his father. "In the mean time, you must try to see things within your own mind."

Mr. Temple then began the following story: -

BENJAMIN WEST.

[BORN 1738. DIED 1820]

In the year 1735 there came into the world, in the town of Springfield, Pennsylvania, a Quaker infant, from whom his parents and neighbors looked for wonderful things. A famous preacher of the Society of Friends had prophesied about little Ben, and foretold that he would be one of the most remarkable characters that, had appeared on the earth since the days of William Penn. On this account the eyes of many people were fixed upon the boy. Some of his ancestors had won great renown in the old wars of England and France; but it was probably expected that Ben would become a preacher, and would convert multitudes to the peaceful doctrines of the Quakers. Friend West and his wife were thought to be very fortunate in having such a son.

Little Ben lived to the ripe age of six years without doing anything that was worthy to be told in history. But one summer afternoon, in his seventh year, his mother put a fan into his hand and bade him keep the flies away from the face of a little babe who lay fast asleep in the cradle. She then left the room.

The boy waved the fan to and fro and drove away the buzzing flies whenever they had the impertinence to come near the baby's face. When they had all flown out of the window or into distant parts of the room, he bent over the cradle and delighted himself with gazing at the sleeping infant. It was, indeed, a very pretty sight. The little personage in the cradle slumbered peacefully, with its waxen hands under its chin, looking as full of blissful quiet as if angels were singing lullabies in its ear. Indeed, it must have been dreaming about heaven; for, while Ben stooped over the cradle, the little baby smiled.

"How beautiful she looks!" said Ben to himself. "What a pity it is that such a pretty smile should not last forever!"

Now Ben, at this period of his life, had never heard of that wonderful art by which a look, that appears and vanishes in a moment, may be made to last for hundreds of years. But, though nobody had told him of such an art, he may be said to have invented it for himself. On a table near at hand there were pens and paper, and ink of two colors, black and red. The boy seized a pen and sheet of paper, and, kneeling down beside the cradle, began to draw a likeness of the infant. While he was busied in this manner he heard his mother's step approaching, and hastily tried to conceal the paper.

"Benjamin, my son, what hast thou been doing?" inquired his mother, observing marks of confusion in his face.

At first Ben was unwilling to tell; for he felt as if there might be something wrong in stealing the baby's face and putting it upon a sheet of paper. However, as his mother insisted, he finally put the sketch into her hand, and then hung his head, expecting to be well scolded. But when the good lady saw what was orn the paper, in lines of red and black ink, she uttered a scream of surprise and joy.

"Bless me!" cried she. "It is a picture of little Sally!"

And then she threw her arms round our friend Benjamin, and kissed him so tenderly that he never afterwards was afraid to show his performances to his mother.

As Ben grew older, he was observed to take vast delight in looking at the lines and forms of nature. For instance, he was greatly pleased with the blue violets of spring, the wild roses of sumnmer, and the scarlet cardinal-flowers of early autumn. In the decline of the year, when the woods were variegated with all the colors of the rainbow, Ben seemed to desire nothing better than to gaze at them from morn till night. The purple and golden clouds of sunset were a joy to him. And he was continually endeavoring to draw the figures of trees, men, mountains, houses, cattle, geese, ducks, and turkeys, with a piece of chalk, on barn doors or on the floor.

In these old times the Mohawk Indians were still numerous in Pennsylvania. Every year a party of them used to pay a visit to Springfield, because the wigwams of their ancestors had formerly stood there. These wild men grew fond of little Ben, and made him very happy by giving him some of the red and yellow paint with which they were accustomed to adorn their faces. His mother, too, presented him with a piece of indigo. Thus he now had three colors, - red, blue, and yellow, - and could manufacture green by mixing the yellow with the blue. Our friend Ben was overjoyed, and doubtless showed his gratitude to the Indians by taking their likenesses in the strange dresses which they wore, with feathers, tomahawks, and bows and arrows.

But all this time the young artist had no paint-brushes;

nor were there any to be bought, unless he had sent to Philadelphia on purpose. However, he was a very ingenious boy, aid resolved to manufacture paint-brushes for himself. With this design he laid hold upon - what do you think? Why, upon a respectable old black cat, who was sleeping quietly by the fireside.

"Puss," said little Ben to the cat, "pray give me some of the fur from the tip of thy tail?"

Though he addressed the black cat so civilly, yet Ben was determined to have the fur whether she were willing or not. Puss, who had no great zeal for the fine arts, would have resisted if she could; but the boy was armed with his mother's scissors, and very dexterously clipped off fur enough to make a paint-brush. This was of so much use to him that be applied to Madame Puss again and again, until her warm coat of fur had become so thin and ragged that she could hardly keep comfortable through the winter. Poor thing! she was forced to creep close into the chimney-corner, and eyed Ben with a very rueful physiognomy. But Ben considered it more necessary that he should have paint-brushes than that puss should be warm.

About this period friend West received a visit from Mr. Pennington, a merchant of Philadelphia, who was likewise a member of the Society of Friends. The visitor, on entering the parlor, was surprised to see it ornamented with drawings of Indian chiefs, and of birds with beautiful plumage, and of the wild flowers of the forest. Nothing of the kind was ever seen before in the habitation of a Quaker farmer.

"Why, Friend West," exclaimed the Philadelphia merchant, "what has possessed thee to cover thy walls with all these pictures? Where on earth didst then get them?"

Then Friend West explained that all these pictures were painted by little Ben, with no better materials than red and yellow ochre and a piece of indigo, and with brushes made of the black cat's fur.

"Verily," said Mr. Pennington, "the boy hath a wonderful faculty. Some of our friends might look upon these matters as vanity; but little Benjamin appears to have been born a painter; and Providence is wiser than we are."

The good merchant patted Benjamin on the head, and evidently considered him a wonderful boy. When his parents saw how much their son's performances were admired, they, no doubt, remembered the prophecy of the old Quaker preacher respecting Ben's future eminence. Yet they could not understand how he was ever to become a very great and useful man merely by making pictures.

One evening, shortly after Mr. Pennington's return to Philadelphia, a package arrived at Springfield, directed to our little friend Ben.

"What can it possibly be?" thought Ben, when it was put into his hands. "Who can have sent me such a great square package as this?"

On taking off the thick brown paper which enveloped it, behold! there was a paint-box, with a great many cakes of paint, and brushes of various sizes. It was the gift of good Mr. Pennington. There were likewise several squares of canvas such as artists use for painting pictures upon, and, in addition to all these treasures, some beautiful engravings of landscapes. These were the first pictures that Ben had ever seen, except those of his own drawing.

What a joyful evening was this for the little artist! At bedtime he put the paint-box under his pillow, and got hardly a wink of sleep; for, all night long, his fancy was painting pictures in the darkness. In the morning he hurried to the garret, and was seen no more till the dinner-hour; nor did he give himself time to eat more than a mouthful or two of food before he hurried back to the garret again. The next day, and the next, he was just as busy as ever; until at last his mother thought it time to ascertain what he was about. She accordingly followed him to the garret.

On opening the door, the first object that presented itself to her eyes was our friend Benjamin, giving the last touches to a beautiful picture. He had copied portions of two of the engravings, and made one picture out of both, with such admirable skill that it was far more beautiful than the originals. The grass, the trees, the water, the sky, and the houses were all painted in their proper colors. There, too, where the sunshine and the shadow, looking as natural as life.

"My dear child, thou hast done wonders!" cried his mother.

The good lady was in an ecstasy of delight. And well might she be proud of her boy; for there were touches in this picture which old artists, who had spent a lifetime in the business, need not have been ashamed of. Many a year afterwards, this wonderful production was exhibited at the Royal Academy in London.

When Benjamin was quite a large lad he was sent to school at Philadelphia. Not long after his arrival he had a slight attack of fever, which confined him to his bed. The light, which would otherwise have disturbed him, was excluded from his chamber by means of closed wooden shutters. At first it appeared so totally dark that Ben could not distinguish any object in the room. By degrees, however, his eyes became accustomed to the scanty light.

He was lying on his back, looking up towards the ceiling, when suddenly he beheld the dim apparition of a white cow moving slowly over his head! Ben started, and rubbed his eyes in the greatest amazement.

"What can this mean?" thought he.

The white cow disappeared; and next came several pigs, which trotted along the ceiling and vanished into the darkness of the chamber. So lifelike did these grunters look that Ben almost seemed to hear them squeak.

"Well, this is very strange!" said Ben to himself.

When the people of the house came to see him, Benjamin told them of the marvellous circumstance which had occurred. But they would not believe him.

"Benjamin, thou art surely out of thy senses!" cried they. "How is it possible that a white cow and a litter of pigs should be visible on the ceiling of a dark chamber?"

Ben, however, had great confidence in his own eyesight, and was determined to search the mystery to the bottom. For this purpose, when he was again left alone, he got out of bed and examined the window-shutters. He soon perceived a small chink in one of them, through which a ray of light found its passage and rested upon the ceiling. Now, the science of optics will inform us that the pictures of the white cow and the pigs, and of other objects out of doors, came into the dark chamber through this narrow chink, and were painted over Benjamin's head. It is greatly to his credit that he discovered the scientific principle of this phenomenon, and by means of it constructed a camera-obscura, or magic-lantern, out of a hollow box. This was of great advantage to him in drawing landscapes.

Well, time went on, and Benjamin continued to draw and paint pictures until he had now reached the age when it was proper that he should choose a business for life. His father and mother were in considerable perplexity about him. According to the ideas of the Quakers, it is not right for people to spend their lives in occupations that are of no real and sensible advantage to the world. Now, what advantage could the world expect from Benjamin's pictures? This was a difficult question; and, in order to set their minds at rest, his parents determined to consult the preachers and wise men of their society. Accordingly, they all assembled in the meeting-house, and discussed the matter from beginning to end.

Finally they came to a very wise decision. It seemed so evident that Providence had created Benjamin to be a painter, and had given him abilities which would be thrown away in any other business, that the Quakers resolved not to oppose his inclination. They even acknowledged that the sight of a beautiful picture might convey instruction to the mind and might benefit the heart as much as a good book or a wise discourse. They therefore committed the youth to the direction of God, being well assured that he best knew what was his proper sphere of usefulness. The old men laid their hands upon Benjamin's head and gave him their blessing, and the women kissed him affectionately. All consented that he should go forth into the world and learn to be a painter by studying the best pictures of ancient and modern times.

So our friend Benjamin left the dwelling of his parents, and his native woods and streams, and the good Quakers of Springfield, and the Indians who had given him his first colors; he left all the places and persons whom he had hitherto known, and returned to them no more. He went first to Philadelphia, and afterwards to Europe. Here he was noticed by many great people, but retained all the sobriety and simplicity which he had learned among the Quakers. It is related of him, that, when he was presented at the court of the Prince of Parma, he kept his hat upon his head even while kissing the Prince's hand.

When he was twenty-five years old he went to London and established himself there as all artist. In due course of time he acquired great fame by his pictures, and was made chief painter to King George III. and president of the Royal Academy of Arts. When the Quakers of Pennsylvania heard of his success, they felt that the prophecy of the old preacher as to little Ben's future eminence was now accomplished. It is true, they shook their heads at his pictures of battle and bloodshed, such as the Death of Wolfe, thinking that these terrible scene, should not be held up to the admiration of the world.

But they approved of the great paintings in which he represented the miracles and sufferings of the Redeemer of mankind. King George employed him to adorn a large and beautiful chapel at Windsor Castle with pictures of these sacred subjects. He likewise painted a magnificent picture of Christ Healing the Sick, which he gave to the hospital at Philadelphia. It was exhibited to the public, and produced so much profit that the hospital was enlarged so as to accommodate thirty more patients. If Benjamin West had done no other good deed than this, yet it would have been enough to entitle him to an honorable remembrance forever. At this very day there are thirty poor people in the hospital who owe all their comforts to that same picture..

We shall mention only a single incident more. The picture of Christ Healing the Sick was exhibited at the Royal Academy in London, where it covered a vast space and displayed a multitude of figures as large as life. On the wall, close beside this admirable picture, hung a small and faded landscape. It was the same that little Ben had painted in his father's garret, after receiving the paint-box and engravings from good Mr. Pennington.

He lived many years in peace and honor, and died in 1820, at the age of eighty-two. The story of his life is almost as wonderful as a fairy tale; for there are few stranger transformations than that of a little unknown Quaker boy, in the wilds of America, into the most distinguished English painter of his day. Let us each make the best use of our natural abilities as Benjamin West did; and, with the blessing of Providence, we shall arrive at some good end. As for fame, it is but little matter whether we acquire it or not.

"Thank you for the story, my dear father," said Edward, when it was finished. "Do you know that it seems as if I could see things without the help of my eyes? While you were speaking I have seen little Bert, and the baby in its cradle, and the Indians, and the white cow, and the pigs, and kind Mr. Pennington, and all the good old Quakers, almost as plainly as if they were in this very room."

"It is because your attention was not disturbed by outward objects," replied Mr. Temple. "People, when deprived of sight, often have more vivid ideas than those who possess the perfect use of their eyes. I will venture to say that George has not attended to the story quite so closely."

"No, indeed," said George; "but it was a very pretty story for all that. How I should have laughed to see Ben making a paint-brush out of the black cat's tail! I intend to try the experiment with Emily's kitten."

"O no, no, George!" cried Emily, earnestly. "My kitten cannot spare her tail."

Edward being an invalid, it was now time for him to retire to bed. When the family bade him good night he turned his face towards them, looking very loath to part.

"I shall not know when morning comes," said he, sorrowfully. "And besides, I want to hear your voices all the time; for, when nobody is speaking, it seems as if I were alone in a dark world."

"You must have faith, my dear child," replied his mother. "Faith is the soul's eyesight; and when we possess it the world is never dark nor lonely."

CHAPTER III.

The next day Edward began to get accustomed to his new condition of life. Once, indeed, when his parents were out of the way and only Emily was left to take care of him, he could not resist the temptation to thrust aside the bandage and peep at the anxious face of his little nurse. But, in spite of the dimness of the chamber, the experiment caused him so much pain that he felt no inclination to take another look. So, with a deep sigh, here signed himself to his fate.

"Emily, pray talk to me!" said he, somewhat impatiently.

Now, Emily was a remarkably silent little girl, and did not possess that liveliness of disposition which renders some children such excellent companions. She seldom laughed, and had not the faculty of making many words about small matters. But the love and earnestness of her heart taught her how to amuse poor Edward in his darkness. She put her knitting-work into his hands.

"You must learn how to knit," said she.

"What! without using my eyes?" cried Edward.

"I can knit with my eyes shut," replied Emily.

Then with her own little hands she guided Edward's fingers while he set about this new occupation. So awkward were his first attempts that any other little girl would have laughed heartily. But Emily preserved her gravity, and showed the utmost patience in taking up the innumerable stitches which he let down. In the course of an hour or two his progress was quite encouraging.

When evening came, Edward acknowledged that the day had been far less wearisome than he anticipated. But he was glad, nevertheless, when his father and mother, and George and Emily, all took their seats around his chair. He put out his hand to grasp each of their hands, and smiled with a very bright expression upon his lips.

"Now I can see you all with my mind's eye," said he. "And now, father, pray tell us another story."

So Mr. Temple began.

SIR ISAAC NEWTON.

[BORN 1642, DIED 1727]

On Christmas day, in the year 1642, Isaac Newton was born at the small village of Woolsthorpe, in England. Little did his mother think, when she beheld her newborn babe, that he was destined to explain many matters which had been a mystery ever since the creation of the world.

Isaac's father being dead, Mrs. Newton was married

again to a clergyman, and went to reside at North Witham. Her son was left to the care of his good old grandmother, who was very kind to him and sent him to school. In his early years Isaac did not appear to be a very bright scholar, but was chiefly remarkable for his ingenuity in all mechanical occupations. He had a set of little tools and saws of various sizes manufactured by himself. With the aid of these Isaac contrived to make many curious articles, at which he worked with so much skill that he seemed to have been born with a saw or chisel in hand.

The neighbors looked with vast admiration at the things which Isaac manufactured. And his old grandmother, I suppose, was never weary of talking about him.

"He'll make a capital workman one of these days," she would probably say. "No fear but what Isaac will do well in the world and be a rich man before he dies."

It is amusing to conjecture what were the anticipations of his grandmother and the neighbors about Isaac's future life. Some of them, perhaps, fancied that he would make beautiful furniture of mahogany, rosewood, or polished oak, inlaid with ivory and ebony, and magnificently gilded. And then, doubtless, all the rich people would purchase these fine things to adorn their drawing-rooms. Others probably thought that little Isaac was destined to be an architect, and would build splendid mansions for the nobility and gentry, and churches too, with the tallest steeples that had ever been seen in England.

Some of his friends, no doubt, advised Isaac's grandmother to apprentice him to a clock-maker; for, besides his mechanical skill, the boy seemed to have a taste for mathematics, which would be very useful to him in that profession. And then, in due time, Isaac would set up for himself, and would manufacture curious clocks, like those that contain sets of dancing figures, which issue from the dial-plate when the hour is struck; or like those where a ship sails across the face of the clock, and is seen tossing up and down on the waves as often as the pendulum vibrates.

Indeed, there was some ground for supposing that Isaac would devote himself to the manufacture of clocks; since he had already made one, of a kind which nobody had ever heard of before. It was set a-going, not by wheels and weights like other clocks, but by the dropping of water. This was an object of great wonderment to all the people round about; and it must be confessed that there are few boys, or men either, who could contrive to tell what o'clock it is by means of a bowl of water.

Besides the water-clock, Isaac made a sundial. Thus his grandmother was never at a loss to know the hour; for the water-clock would tell it in the shade, and the dial in the sunshine. The sundial is said to be still in existence at Woolsthorpe, on the corner of the house where Isaac dwelt. If so, it must have marked the passage of every sunny hour that has elapsed since Isaac Newton was a boy. It marked all the famous moments of his life; it marked the hour of his death; and still the sunshine creeps slowly over it, as regularly as when Isaac first set it up.

Yet we must not say that the sundial has lasted longer than its maker; for Isaac Newton will exist long after the dial - yes, and long after the sun itself - shall have crumbled to decay.

Isaac possessed a wonderful faculty of acquiring knowledge by the simplest means. For instance, what method do you suppose he took to find out the strength of the wind? You will never guess how the boy could compel that unseen, inconstant, and ungovernable wonder, the wind, to tell him the measure of its strength. Yet nothing can be more simple. He jumped against the wind; and by the length of his jump he could calculate the force of a gentle breeze, a brisk gale, or a tempest. Thus, even in his boyish sports, he was continually searching out the secrets of philosophy.

Not far from his grandmother's residence there was a windmill which operated on a new plan. Isaac was in the habit of going thither frequently, and would spend whole hours in examining its various parts. While the mill was at rest he pried into its internal machinery. When its broad sails were set in motion by the wind, he watched the process by which the mill-stones were made to revolve and crush the grain that was put into the hopper. After gaining a thorough knowledge of its construction he was observed to be unusually busy with his tools.

It was not long before his grandmother and all the neighborhood knew what Isaac had been about. He had constructed a model of the windmill. Though not so large, I suppose, as one of the box traps which boys set to catch squirrels, yet every part of the mill and is machinery was complete. Its little sails were neatly made of linen, and whirled round very swiftly when the mill was placed in a draught of air. Even a puff of wind from Isaac's mouth or from a pair of bellows was sufficient to set the sails in motion. And, what was most curious, if a handful of grains of wheat were put into the little hopper, they would soon be converted into snow-white flour.

Isaac's playmates were enchanted with his new windmill. They thought that nothing so pretty and so wonderful had ever been seen in the whole world.

"But, Isaac," said one of them, "you have forgotten one thing that belongs to a mill."

"What is that?" asked Isaac; for he supposed that, from the roof of the mill to its foundation, be had forgotten nothing.

"Why, where is the miller?" said his friend.

"That is true, - I must look out for one," said Isaac; and he set himself to consider how the deficiency should be supplied.

He might easily have made the miniature figure of a man; but then it would not have been able to move about and perform the duties of a miller. As Captain Lemuel Gulliver had not yet discovered the island of Lilliput, Isaac did not know that there were little men in the world whose size was just suited to his windmill. It so happened, however, that a mouse had just been caught in the trap; and, as no other miller could be found, Mr. Mouse was appointed to that important office. The new miller made a very respectable appearance in his dark gray coat. To be sure, he had not a very good character for honesty, and was suspected of sometimes stealing a portion of the grain which was given him to grind. But perhaps some two-legged millers are quite as dishonest as this small quadruped.

As Isaac grew older, it was found that he had far more important matters in his mind than the manufacture of toys like the little windmill. All day long, if left to himself, he was either absorbed in thought or engaged in some book of mathematics or natural philosophy. At night, I think it probable, he looked up with reverential curiosity to the stars, and wondered whether they were worlds like our own, and how great was their distance from the earth, and what was the power that kept them in their courses. Perhaps, even so early in life, Isaac Newton felt a presentiment that he should be able, hereafter, to answer all these questions.

When Isaac was fourteen years old, his mother's second husband being now dead, she wished her son to leave school and assist her in managing the farm at Woolsthorpe. For a year or two, therefore, he tried to turn his attention to farming. But his mind was so bent on becoming a scholar that his mother sent him back to school, and afterwards to the University of Cambridge.

I have now finished my anecdotes of Isaac Newton's boyhood. My story would be far too long were I to mention all the splendid discoveries which he made after he came to be a man. He was the first that found out the nature of light; for, before his day, nobody could tell what the sunshine was composed of. You remember, I suppose, the story of an apple's falling on his head, and thus leading him to discover the force of gravitation, which keeps the heavenly bodies in their courses. When he had once got hold of this idea, he never permitted his mind to rest until he had searched out all the laws by which the planets are guided through the sky. This he did as thoroughly as if he had gone up among the stars and tracked them in their orbits. The boy had found out the mechanism of a windmill; the man explained to his fellow-men the mechanism of the universe.

While making these researches he was accustomed to spend night after night in a lofty tower, gazing at the heavenly bodies through a telescope. His mind was lifted far above the things of this world. He may be said, indeed, to have spent the greater part of his life in worlds that lie thousands and millions of miles away; for where the thoughts and the heart are, there is our true existence.

Did you never hear the story of Newton and his little dog Diamond? One day, when he was fifty years old, and had been hard at work more than twenty years studying the theory of light, he went out of his chamber, leaving his little dog asleep before the fire. On the table lay a heap of manuscript papers, containing all the discoveries which Newton had made during those twenty years. When his master was gone, up rose little Diamond, jumped upon the table, and overthrew the lighted candle. The papers immediately caught fire.

Just as the destruction was completed Newton opened the chamber door, and perceived that the labors of twenty years were reduced to a heap of ashes. There stood little Diamond, the author of all the mischief. Almost any other man would have sentenced the dog to immediate death. But Newton patted him on the head with his usual kindness, although grief was at his heart.

"O Diamond, Diamond," exclaimed he, "thou little knowest the mischief then hast done!"

This incident affected his health and spirits for some time afterwards; but, from his conduct towards the little dog, you may judge what was the sweetness of his temper.

Newton lived to be a very old man, and acquired great renown, and was made a member of Parliament, and received the honor of knighthood from the king. But he cared little for earthly fame and honors, and felt no pride in the vastness of his knowledge. All that he had learned only made him feel how little he knew in comparison to what remained to be known.

"I seem to myself like a child," observed he, "playing on the sea-shore, and picking up here and there a curious shell or a pretty pebble, while the boundless ocean of Truth lies undiscovered before me."

At last, in 1727, when he was fourscore and five years old, Sir Isaac Newton died, - or rather, he ceased to live on earth. We may be permitted to believe that he is still searching out the infinite wisdom and goodness of the Creator as earnestly, and with even more success, than while his spirit animated a mortal body. He has left a fame behind him which will be as endurable as if his name were written in letters of light formed by the stars upon the midnight sky.

"I love to hear about mechanical contrivances, such as the water-clock and the little windmill," remarked George. "I suppose, if Sir Isaac Newton had only thought of it, he might have found out the steam-engine, and railroads, and all the other famous inventions that have come into use since his day."

"Very possibly he might," replied Mr. Temple; "and no doubt a great many people would think it more useful to manufacture steam-engines than to search out the system of the universe. Other great astronomers besides Newton have been endowed with mechanical genius. There was David Rittenhouse, an American, - lie made a perfect little water-mill when he was only seven or eight years old. But this sort of ingenuity is but a mere trifle in comparison with the other talents of such men."

"It must have deen beautiful," said Edward, "to spend whole nights in a high tower as Newton did, gazing at the stars, and the comets, and the meteors. But what would Newton have done had he been blind? or if his eyes had been no better than mine?"

"Why, even then, my dear child," observed Mrs. Temple, "he would have found out some way of enlightening his mind and of elevating his soul. But come; little Emily is waiting to bid you good night. You must go to sleep and dream of seeing all our faces."

"But how sad it will be when I awake!" murmured Edward.

CHAPTER IV.

In the course of the next day the harmony of our little family was disturbed by something like a quarrel between George and Edward.

The former, though he loved his brother dearly, had found it quite too great a sacrifice of his own enjoyments to spend all his play-time in a darkened chamber. Edward, on the other hand, was inclined to be despotic. He felt as if his bandaged eyes entitled him to demand that everybody who enjoyed the blessing of sight should contribute to his comfort and amusement. He therefore insisted that George, instead of going out to play at football, should join with himself and Emily in a game of questions and answers.

George resolutely refused, and ran out of the house. He did not revisit Edward's chamber till the evening, when he stole in, looking confused, yet somewhat sullen, and sat down beside his father's chair. It was evident, by a motion of Edward's head and a slight trembling of his lips, that he was aware of George's entrance, though his footsteps had been almost inaudible. Emily, with her serious and earnest little face, looked from one to the other, as if she longed to be a messenger of peace between them.

Mr. Temple, without seeming to notice any of these circumstances, began a story.

SAMUEL JOHNSON

[BORN 1709 DIED 1784.]

"Sam," said Mr. Michael Johnson, of Lichfield, one morning, "I am very feeble and ailing to-day. You must go to Uttoxeter in my stead, and tend the bookstall in the market-place there."

This was spoken above a hundred years ago, by an elderly man, who had once been a thriving bookseller at Lichfield, in England. Being now in reduced circumstances, he was forced to go every market-day and sell books at a stall, in the neighboring village of Uttoxeter.

His son, to whom Mr. Johnson spoke, was a great boy, of very singular aspect. He had an intelligent face; but it was seamed and distorted by a scrofulous humor, which affected his eyes so badly that sometimes he was almost blind. Owing to the same cause his head would often shake with a tremulous motion as if he were afflicted with the palsy. When Sam was an infant, the famous Queen Anne had tried to cure him of this disease by laying her royal hands upon his head. But though the touch of a king or queen was supposed to be a certain remedy for scrofula, it produced no good effect upon Sam Johnson.

At the time which we speak of the poor lad was not very well dressed, and wore shoes from which his toes peeped out; for his old father had barely the means of supporting his wife and children. But, poor as the family were, young Sam Johnson had as much pride as any nobleman's son in England. The fact was, he felt conscious of uncommon sense and ability, which, in his own opinion, entitled him to great respect from the world. Perhaps he would have been glad if grown people had treated him as reverentially as his schoolfellows did. Three of them were accustomed to come for him every morning; and while he sat upon the back of one, the two others supported him on each side; and thus he rode to school in triumph.

Being a personage of so much importance, Sam could not bear the idea of standing all day in Uttoxeter market offering books to the rude and ignorant country people. Doubtless he felt the more reluctant on account of his shabby clothes, and the disorder of his eyes, and the tremulous motion of his head.

When Mr. Michael Johnson spoke, Sam pouted and made an indistinct grumbling in his throat; then he looked his old father in the face and answered him loudly and deliberately.

"Sir," said he, "I will not go to Uttoxeter market!"

Mr. Johnson had seen a great deal of the lad's obstinacy ever since his birth; and while Sam was younger, the old gentleman had probably used the rod whenever occasion seemed to require. But he was now too feeble and too much out of spirits to contend with this stubborn and violent-tempered boy. He therefore gave up the point at once, and prepared to go to Uttoxeter himself.

"Well, Sam," said Mr. Johnson, as he took his hat and staff, "if for the sake of your foolish pride you can suffer your poor sick father to stand all day in the noise and confusion of the market when he ought to be in his bed, I have no more to say. But you will think of this, Sam, when I am dead and gone."

So the poor old man (perhaps with a tear in his eye, but certainly with sorrow in his heart) set forth towards Uttoxeter. The gray-haired, feeble, melancholy Michael Johnson! How sad a thing it was that he should be forced to go, in his sickness, and toil for the support of an ungrateful son who was too proud to do anything for his father, or his mother, or himself! Sam looked after Mr. Johnson with a sullen countenance till he was out of sight.

But when the old man's figure, as he went stooping along the street, was no more to be seen, the boy's heart began to smite him. He had a vivid imagination, and it tormented him with the image of his father standing in the market-place of Uttoxeter and offering his books to the noisy crowd around him. Sam seemed to behold him arranging his literary merchandise upon the stall in such a way as was best calculated to attract notice. Here was Addison's Spectator, a long row of little volumes; here was Pope's translation of the Iliad and Odyssey; here were Dryden's poems, or those of Prior. Here, likewise, were Gulliver's Travels, and a variety of little gilt-covered children's books, such as Tom Thumb, Jack the Giant Queller, Mother Goose's Melodies, and others which our great-grandparents used to read in their childhood. And here were sermons for the pious, and pamphlets for the politicians, and ballads, some merry and some dismal ones, for the country people to sing.

Sam, in imagination, saw his father offer these books, pamphlets, and ballads, now to the rude yeomen who perhaps could not read a word; now to the country squires, who cared for nothing but to hunt hares and foxes; now to the children, who chose to spend their coppers for sugar-plums or gingerbread rather than for picture-books. And if Mr. Johnson should sell a book to man, woman, or child, it would cost him an hour's talk to get a profit of only sixpence.

"My poor father!" thought Sam to himself. "How his head will ache! and how heavy his heart will be! I am almost sorry that I did not do as he bade me."

Then the boy went to his mother, who was busy about the house. She did not know of what had passed between Mr. Johnson and Sam.

"Mother," said he, "did you think father seemed very ill to-day?"

"Yes, Sam," answered his mother, turning with a flushed face from the fire, where she was cooking their scanty dinner. "Your father did look very ill; and it is a pity he did not send you to Uttoxeter in his stead. You are a great boy now, and would rejoice, I am sure, to do something for your poor father, who has done so much for you."

The lad made no reply. But again his imagination set to work and conjured up another picture of poor Michael Johnson. He was standing in the hot sunshine of the market-place, and looking so weary, sick, and disconsolate, that the eyes of all the crowd were drawn to him. "Had this old man no son," the people would say among themselves, "who might have taken his place at the bookstall while the father kept his bed?" And perhaps, but this was a terrible thought for Sam! - perhaps his father would faint away and fall down in the marketplace, with his gray hair in the dust and his venerable face as deathlike as that of a corpse. And there would be the bystanders gazing earnestly at Mr. Johnson and whispering, "Is he dead? Is he dead?"

And Sam shuddered as he repeated to himself, "Is he dead?"

"O, I have been a cruel son!" thought he, within his own heart. "God forgive me! God forgive me!"

But God could not yet forgive him; for he was not truly penitent. Had he been so, he would have hastened away that very moment to Uttoxeter, and have fallen at his father's feet, even in the midst of the crowded market-place. There he would have confessed his fault, and besought Mr. Johnson to go home and leave the rest of the day's work to him. But such was Sam's pride and natural stubbornness that he could not bring himself to this humiliation. Yet he ought to have done so, for his own sake, for his father's sake, and for God's sake.

After sunset old Michael Johnson came slowly home and sat down in his customary chair. He said nothing to Sam; nor do I know that a single word ever passed between them on the subject of the son's disobedience. In a few years his father died, and left Sam to fight his way through the world by himself. It would make our story much too long were I to tell you even a few of the remarkable events of Sam's life. Moreover, there is the less need of this, because many books have been written about that poor boy, and the fame that he acquired, and all that he did or talked of doing after he came to be a man.

But one thing I must not neglect to say. From his boyhood upward until the latest day of his life he never forgot the story of Uttoxeter market. Often when he was a scholar of the University of Oxford, or master of an academy at Edial, or a writer for the London booksellers, - in all his poverty and toil and in all his success, - while he was walking the streets without a shilling to buy food, or when the greatest men of England were proud to feast him at their table, - still that heavy and remorseful thought came back to him, "I was cruel to my poor father in his illness!" Many and many a time, awake or in his dreams, he seemed to see old Michael Johnson standing in the dust and confusion of the market-place and pressing his withered hand to his forehead as if it ached.

Alas! my dear children, it is a sad thing to have such a thought as this to bear us company through life.

Though the story was but half finished, yet, as it was longer than usual, Mr. Temple here made a short pause. He perceived that Emily was in tears, and Edward turned his half-veiled face towards the speaker with an air of great earnestness and interest. As for George, he had withdrawn into the dusky shadow behind his father's chair.

CHAPTER V.

In a few moments Mr. Temple resumed the story, as follows: -

SAMUEL JOHNSON.

[CONTINUED]

Well, my children, fifty years had passed away since young Sam Johnson had shown himself so hard-hearted towards his father. It was now market-day in the village of Uttoxeter.

In the street of the village you might see cattle-dealers with cows and oxen for sale, and pig-drovers with herds of squeaking swine, and farmers with cartloads of cabbages, turnips, onions, and all other produce of the soil. Now and then a farmer's red-faced wife trotted along on horseback, with butter and cheese in two large panniers. The people of the village, with country squires, and other visitors from the neighborhood, walked hither and thither, trading, jesting, quarrelling, and making just such a bustle as their fathers and grandfathers had made half a century before.

In one part of the street there was a puppet-show with a ridiculous merry-andrew, who kept both grown people and children in a roar of laughter. On the opposite side was the old stone church of Uttoxeter, with ivy climbing up its walls and partly obscuring its Gothic windows.

There was a clock in the gray tower of the ancient church, and the hands on the dial-plate had now almost reached the hour of noon. At this busiest hour of the market a strange old gentleman was seen making his way among the crowd, he was very tall and bulky, and wore a brown coat and small-clothes, with black worsted stockings and buckled shoes. On his head was a three cornered hat, beneath which a bushy gray wig thrust itself out, all in disorder. The old gentleman elbowed the people aside, and forced his way through the midst of them with a singular kind of gait, rolling his body hither and thither, so that he needed twice as much room as any other person there.

"Make way, sir!" he would cry out, in a loud, harsh voice, when somebody happened to interrupt his progress. "Sir, you intrude your person into the public thoroughfare!"

"What a queer old fellow this is!" muttered the people among themselves, hardly knowing whether to laugh or to be angry.

But when they looked into the venerable stranger's face, not the most thoughtless among them dared to offer him the least impertinence. Though his features were scarred and distorted with the scrofula, and though his eyes were dim and bleared, yet there was something of authority and wisdom in his look, which impressed them all with awe. So they stood aside to let him pass; and the old gentleman made his way across the market-place, and paused near the corner of the ivy-mantled church. Just as he reached it the clock struck twelve.

On the very spot of ground where the stranger now stood some aged people remembered that old Michael Johnson had formerly kept his book-stall. The little children who had once bought picture-books of him were grandfathers now.

"Yes; here is the very spot!" muttered the old gentleman to himself.

There this unknown personage took his stand and removed the three-cornered hat from his head. It was the busiest hour of the day. What with the hum of human voices, the lowing of cattle, the squeaking of pigs, and the laughter caused by the merry-andrew, the marketplace was in very great confusion. But the stranger seemed not to notice it any more than if the silence of a desert were around him. He was rapt in his own thoughts. Sometimes he raised his furrowed brow to heaven, as if in prayer; sometimes he bent his head, as if an insupportable weight of sorrow were upon him. It increased the awfulness of his aspect that there was a motion of his head and an almost continual tremor throughout his frame, with singular twitches and contortions of his features. The hot sun blazed upon his unprotected head; but he seemed not to feel its fervor. A dark cloud swept across the sky and rain-drops pattered into the market-place; but the stranger heeded not the shower. The people began to gaze at the mysterious old gentleman with superstitious fear and wonder. Who could he be? Whence did he come? Wherefore was he standing bareheaded in the market-place? Even the school-boys left the merry-andrew and came to gaze, with wide-open eyes, at this tall, strange-looking old man.

There was a cattle-drover in the village who had recently made a journey to the Smithfield market, in London. No sooner had this man thrust his way through the throng and taken a look at the unknown personage, than he whispered to one of his acquaintances, -

"I say, Neighbor Hutchins, would ye like to know who this old gentleman is?"

"Ay, that I would," replied Neighbor Hutchins, "for a queerer chap I never saw in my life. Somehow it makes me feel small to look at him. He's more than a common man."

"You may well say so," answered the cattle-drover. "Why, that's the famous Doctor Samuel Johnson, who they say is the greatest and learnedest man in England. I saw him in London streets, walking with one Mr. Boswell."

Yes; the poor boy, the friendless Sam, with whom we began our story, had become the famous Doctor Samuel Johnson. He was universally acknowledged as the wisest man and greatest writer in all England. He had given shape and permanence to his native language by his Dictionary. Thousands upon thousands of people had read his Idler, his Rambler, and his Rasselas. Noble and wealthy men and beautiful ladies deemed it their highest privilege to be his companions. Even the King of Great Britain had sought his acquaintance, and told him what an honor he considered it that such a man had been born in his dominions. He was now at the summit of literary renown.

But all his fame could not extinguish the bitter remembrance which had tormented him through life. Never never had he forgotten his father's sorrowful and upbraiding look. Never, though the old man's troubles had been over so many years, had he forgiven himself for inflicting such a pang upon his heart. And now, in his old age, he had come hither to do penance, by standing at noonday, in the market-place of Uttoxeter, on the very spot where Michael Johnson had once kept his book-stall. The aged and illustrious man had done what the poor boy refused to do. By thus expressing his deep repentance and humiliation of heart, he hoped to gain peace of conscience and the forgiveness of God.

My dear children, if you have grieved (I will not say your parents, but if you have grieved) the heart of any human being who has a claim upon your love, then think of Samuel Johnson's penance. Will it not be better to redeem the error now than to endure the agony of remorse for fifty years? Would you not rather say to a brother, "I have erred; forgive me!" than perhaps to go hereafter and shed bitter tears upon his grave?

Hardly was the story concluded when George hastily arose, and Edward likewise, stretching forth his hands into the darkness that surrounded him to find his brother. Both accused themselves of unkindness: each besought the other's forgiveness; and having done so, the trouble of their hearts vanished away like a dream.

"I am glad! I am so glad!" said Emily, in a low, earnest voice. "Now I shall sleep quietly to-night."

"My sweet child," thought Mrs. Temple as she kissed

her, "mayest thou never know how much strife there is on earth! It would cost thee many a night's rest."

CHAPTER VI.

About this period Mr. Temple found it necessary to take a journey, which interrupted the series of Biographical Stories for several evenings. In the interval, Edward practised various methods of employing and amusing his mind.

Sometimes he meditated upon beautiful objects which he had formerly seen, until the intensity of his recollection seemed to restore him the gift of sight and place everything anew before his eyes. Sometimes he repeated verses of poetry which he did not know to be in his memory until he found them there just at the time of need. Sometimes he attempted to solve arithmetical questions which had perplexed him while at school.

Then, with his mother's assistance, he learned the letters of the string alphabet, which is used in some of the institutions for the blind in Europe. When one of his friends gave him a leaf of St. Mark's Gospel, printed in embossed characters, he endeavored to read it by passing his fingers over the letters as blind children do.

His brother George was now very kind, and spent so much time in the darkened chamber that Edward often insisted upon his going out to play. George told him all about the affairs at school, and related many amusing incidents that happened among his comrades, and informed him what sports were now in fashion, and whose kite soared the highest, and whose little ship sailed fleetest on the Frog Pond. As for Emily, she repeated stories which she had learned from a new book called THE FLOWER PEOPLE, in which the snowdrops, the violets, the columbines, the roses, and all that lovely tribe are represented as telling their secrets to a little girl. The flowers talked sweetly, as flowers should; and Edward almost fancied that he could behold their bloom and smell their fragrant breath.

Thus, in one way or another, the dark days of Edward's confinement passed not unhappily. In due time his father returned; and the next evening, when the family were assembled, he began a story.

"I must first observe, children," said he, "that some writers deny the truth of the incident which I am about to relate to you. There certainly is but little evidence in favor of it. Other respectable writers, however, tell it for a fact; and, at all events, it is an interesting story, and has an excellent moral."

So Mr. Temple proceeded to talk about the early days of

OLIVER CROMWELL.

[BORN 1599 DIED 1658.]

Not long after King James I. took the place of Queen Elizabeth on the throne of England, there lived an English knight at a place called Hinchinbrooke. His name was Sir Oliver Cromwell. He spent his life, I suppose, pretty much like other English knights and squires in those days, bunting hares and foxes and drinking large quantities of ale and wine. The old house in which he dwelt had been occupied by his ancestors before him for a good many years. In it there was a great hall, hang round with coats of arms and helmets, cuirasses and swords, which his forefathers had used in battle, and with horns of deer and tails of foxes which they or Sir Oliver himself had killed in the chase.

This Sir Oliver Cromwell had a nephew, who had been called Oliver, after himself, but who was generally known in the family by the name of little Noll. His father was a younger brother of Sir Oliver. The child was often sent to visit his uncle, who probably found him a troublesome little fellow to take care of. He was forever in mischief, and always running into some danger or other, from which he seemed to escape only by miracle.

Even while he was an infant in the cradle a strange accident had befallen hum. A huge ape, which was kept in the family, snatched up little Noll in his fore paws and clambered with him to the roof of the house. There this ugly beast sat grinning at the affrighted spectators, as if it had done the most praiseworthy thing imaginable. Fortunately, however, he brought the child safe down again; and the event was afterwards considered an omen that Noll would reach a very elevated station in the world.

One morning, when Noll was five or six years old a royal messenger arrived at Hinchinbrooke with tidings that King James was coming to dine with Sir Oliver

Cromwell. This was a high honor, to be sure, but a very great trouble; for all the lords and ladies, knights, squires, guards and yeomen, who waited on the king, were to be feasted as well as himself; and more provisions would be eaten and more wine drunk in that one day than generally in a month. However, Sir Oliver expressed much thankfulness for the king's intended visit, and ordered his butler and cook to make the best preparations in their power. So a great fire was kindled in the kitchen; and the neighbors knew by the smoke which poured out of the chimney that boiling, baking, stewing, roasting, and frying were going on merrily.

By and by the sound of trumpets was heard approaching nearer and nearer; a heavy, old-fashioned coach, surrounded by guards on horseback, drove up to the house. Sir Oliver, with his hat in his hand, stood at the gate to receive the king. His Majesty was dressed in a suit of green not very new; he had a feather in his hat and a triple ruff round his neck, and over his shoulder was slung a hunting-horn instead of a sword. Altogether he had not the most dignified aspect in the world; but the spectators gazed at him as if there was something superhuman and divine in his person. They even shaded their eyes with their hands, as if they were dazzled by the glory of his countenance.

"How are ye, man?" cried King James, speaking in a Scotch accent; for Scotland was his native country. "By my crown, Sir Oliver, but I am glad to see ye!"

The good knight thanked the king; at the same time kneeling down while his Majesty alighted. When King James stood on the ground, he directed Sir Oliver's attention to a little boy who had come with him in the coach. He was six or seven years old, and wore a hat and feather, and was more richly dressed than the king himself. Though by no means an ill-looking child, he seemed shy, or even sulky; and his cheeks were rather pale, as if he had been kept moping within doors, instead of being sent out to play in the sun and wind.

"I have brought my son Charlie to see ye," said the king. "I hope, Sir Oliver, ye have a son of your own to be his playmate."

Sir Oliver Cromwell made a reverential bow to the little prince, whom one of the attendants had now taken out of the coach. It was wonderful to see how all the spectators, even the aged men with their gray beards, humbled themselves before this child. They bent their bodies till their beards almost swept the dust: They looked as if they were ready to kneel down and worship him.

The poor little prince! From his earliest infancy not a soul had dared to contradict him; everybody around him had acted as if he were a superior being; so that, of course, he had imbibed the same opinion of himself. He naturally supposed that the whole kingdom of Great Britain and all its inhabitants had been created solely for his benefit and amusement. This was a sad mistake; and it cost him dear enough after he had ascended his father's throne.

"What a noble little prince he is!" exclaimed Sir Oliver, lifting his hands in admiration. "No, please your Majesty, I have no son to be the playmate of his royal highness; but there is a nephew of mine somewhere about the house. He is near the prince's age, and will be but too happy to wait upon his royal highness."

"Send for him, man! send for him!" said the king.

But, as it happened, there was no need of sending for Master Noll. While King James was speaking, a rugged, bold-faced, sturdy little urchin thrust himself through the throng of courtiers and attendants and greeted the prince with a broad stare. His doublet and hose (which had been put on new and clean in honor of the king's visit) were already soiled and torn with the rough play in which he had spent the morning. He looked no more abashed than if King James were his uncle and the prince one of his customary playfellows.

This was little Noll himself.

"Here, please your Majesty, is my nephew," said Sir Oliver, somewhat ashamed of Noll's appearance and demeanor. "Oliver, make your obeisance to the king's majesty."

The boy made a pretty respectful obeisance to the king; for in those days children were taught to pay reverence to their elders. King James, who prided himself greatly on his scholarship, asked Noll a few questions in the Latin grammar, and then introduced him to his son. The little prince, in a very grave and dignified manner, extended his hand, not for Noll to shake, but that he might kneel down and kiss it.

"Nephew," said Sir Oliver, "pay your duty to the prince."

"I owe him no duty," cried Noll, thrusting aside the

prince's hand with a rude laugh. "Why should I kiss that boy's hand?"

All the courtiers were amazed and confounded, and Sir Oliver the most of all. But the king laughed heartily, saying, that little Noll had a stubborn English spirit, and that it was well for his son to learn betimes what sort of a people he was to rule over.

So King James and his train entered the house; and the prince, with Noll and some other children, was sent to play in a separate room while his Majesty was at dinner. The young people soon became acquainted; for boys, whether the sons of monarchs or of peasants, all like play, and are pleased with one another's society. What games they diverted themselves with I cannot tell. Perhaps they played at ball, perhaps at blindman's-buff, perhaps at leap-frog, perhaps at prison-bars. Such games have been in use for hundreds of years; and princes as well as poor children have spent some of their happiest hours in playing at them.

Meanwhile King James and his nobles were feasting with Sir Oliver in the great hall. The king sat in a gilded chair, under a canopy, at the head of a long table. Whenever any of the company addressed him, it was with the deepest reverence. If the attendants offered him wine or the various delicacies of the festival, it was upon their bended knees. You would have thought, by these tokens of worship, that the monarch was a supernatural being; only he seemed to have quite as much need of those vulgar matters, food and drink, as any other person at the table. But fate had ordained that good King James should not finish his dinner in peace.

All of a sudden there arose a terrible uproar in the room where the children were at play. Angry shouts and shrill cries of alarm were mixed up together; while the voices of elder persons were likewise heard, trying to restore order among the children. The king and everybody else at table looked aghast; for perhaps the tumult made them think that a general rebellion had broken out.

"Mercy on us!" muttered Sir Oliver; "that graceless nephew of mine is in some mischief or other. The naughty little whelp!"

Getting up from table, he ran to see what was the matter, followed by many of the guests, and the king among them. They all crowded to the door of the playroom.

On looking in, they beheld the little Prince Charles, with his rich dress all torn and covered with the dust of the floor. His royal blood was streaming from his nose in great abundance. He gazed at Noll with a mixture of rage and affright, and at the same time a puzzled expression, as if he could not understand how any mortal boy should dare to give him a beating. As for Noll, there stood his sturdy little figure, bold as a lion, looking as if he were ready to fight, not only the prince, but the king and kingdom too.

"You little villain!" cried his uncle. "What have you been about? Down on your knees, this instant, and ask the prince's pardon. How dare you lay your hands on the king's majesty's royal son?"

"He struck me first," grumbled the valiant little Noll; "and I've only given him his due."

Sir Oliver and the guests lifted up their hands in astonishment and horror. No punishment seemed severe enough for this wicked little varlet, who had dared to resent a blow from the king's own son. Some of the courtiers were of opinion that Noll should be sent prisoner to the Tower of London and brought to trial for high treason. Others, in their great zeal for the king's service, were about to lay hands on the boy and chastise him in the royal presence.

But King James, who sometimes showed a good deal of sagacity, ordered them to desist.

"Thou art a bold boy," said he, looking fixedly at little Noll; "and, if thou live to be a man, my son Charlie would do wisely to be friends with thee."

"I never will!" cried the little prince, stamping his foot.

"Peace, Charlie, peace!" said the king; then addressing Sir Oliver and the attendants, "Harm not the urchin; for he has taught my son a good lesson, if Heaven do but give him grace to profit by it. Hereafter, should he be tempted to tyrannize over the stubborn race of Englishmen, let him remember little Noll Cromwell and his own bloody nose."

So the king finished his dinner and departed; and for many a long year the childish quarrel between Prince Charles and Noll Cromwell was forgotten. The prince, indeed, might have lived a happier life, and have met a more peaceful death, had he remembered that quarrel and the moral which his father drew from it. But when old King James was dead, and Charles sat upon his throne, he seemed to forget that he was but a man, and that his meanest subjects were men as well as he. He wished to have the property and lives of the people of England entirely at his own disposal. But the Puritans, and all who loved liberty, rose against him and beat him in many battles, and pulled him down from his throne.

Throughout this war between the king and nobles on one side and the people of England on the other there was a famous leader, who did more towards the ruin of royal authority than all the rest. The contest seemed like a wrestling-match between King Charles and this strong man. And the king was overthrown.

When the discrowned monarch was brought to trial, that warlike leader sat in the judgment hall. Many judges were present besides himself; but he alone had the power to save King Charles or to doom him to the scaffold. After sentence was pronounced, this victorious general was entreated by his own children, on their knees, to rescue his Majesty from death.

"No!" said he, sternly. "Better that one man should perish than that the whole country should be ruined for his sake. It is resolved that he shall die!"

When Charles, no longer a king, was led to the scaffold, his great enemy stood at a window of the royal palace of Whitehall. He beheld the poor victim of pride, and an evil education, and misused power, as he laid his head upon the block. He looked on with a steadfast gaze while a black-veiled executioner lifted the fatal axe and smote off that anointed head at a single blow.

"It is a righteous deed," perhaps he said to himself.

"Now Englishmen may enjoy their rights."

At night, when the body of Charles was laid in the coffin, in a gloomy chamber, the general entered, lighting himself with a torch. Its gleams showed that he was now growing old; his visage was scarred with the many battles in which he had led the van; his brow was wrinkled with care and with the continual exercise of stern authority. Probably there was not a single trait, either of aspect or manner, that belonged to the little Noll who had battled so stoutly with Prince Charles. Yet this was he!

He lifted the coffin-lid, and caused the light of his torch to fall upon the dead monarch's face. Then, probably, his mind went back over all the marvellous events that had brought the hereditary King of England to this dishonored coffin, and had raised himself, a humble individual, to the possession of kingly power. He was a king, though without the empty title or the glittering crown.

"Why was it," said Cromwell to himself, or might have said, as he gazed at the pale features in the coffin, - "why was it that this great kingfell, and that poor Noll Cromwell has gained all the power of the realm?"

And, indeed, why was it?

King Charles had fallen, because, in his manhood the same as when a child, he disdained to feel that every human creature was his brother. He deemed himself a superior being, and fancied that his subjects were created only for a king to rule over. And Cromwell rose, because, in spite of his many faults, he mainly fought for the rights and freedom of his fellow-men;

and therefore the poor and the oppressed all lent their strength to him.

"Dear father, how I should hate to be a king!" exclaimed Edward.

"And would you like to be a Cromwell?" inquired his father.

"I should like it well," replied George; "only I would not have put the poor old king to death. I would have sent him out of the kingdom, or perhaps have allowed him to live in a small house near the gate of the royal palace. It was too severe to cut off his head."

"Kings are in such an unfortunate position," said Mr. Temple, "that they must either be almost deified by their subjects, or else be dethroned and beheaded. In either case it is a pitiable lot."

"O, I had rather be blind than be a king!" said Edward.

"Well, my dear Edward," observed his mother, with a smile, "I am glad you are convinced that your own lot is not the hardest in the world."

CHAPTER VII.

It was a pleasant sight, for those who had eyes, to see how patiently the blinded little boy now submitted to what he had at first deemed an intolerable calamity. The beneficent Creator has not allowed our comfort to depend on the enjoyment of any single sense. Though he has made the world so very beautiful, yet it is possible to be happy without ever be holding the blue sky, or the green and flowery earth, or the kind faces of those whom we love. Thus it appears that all the external beauty of the universe is a free gift from God over and above what is necessary to our comfort. How grateful, then, should we be to that divine Benevolence, which showers even superfluous bounties upon us!

One truth, therefore, which Edward's blindness had taught him was, that his mind and soul could dispense with the assistance of his eyes. Doubtless, however, he would have found this lesson far more difficult to learn had it not been for the affection of those around him. His parents, and George and Emily, aided him to bear his misfortune; if possible, they would have lent him their own eyes. And this, too, was a good lesson for him. It taught him how dependent on one another God has ordained us to be, insomuch that all the necessities of mankind should incite them to mutual love.

So Edward loved his friends, and perhaps all the world, better than he ever did before. And be felt grateful towards his father for spending the evenings in telling him stories, - more grateful, probably, than any of my little readers will feel towards me for so carefully writing these same stories down.

"Come, dear father," said he, the next evening, "now tell us about some other little boy who was destined to be a famous man."

"How would you like a story of a Boston boy?" asked his father.

"O, pray let us have it!" cried George, eagerly. "It will be all the better if he has been to our schools, and has coasted on the Common, and sailed boats in the Frog Pond. I shall feel acquainted with him. then."

"Well, then," said Mr. Temple, "I will introduce you to a Boston boy whom all the world became acquainted with after he grew to be a man."

The story was as follows: -

BENJAMIN FRANKLIN.

[BORN 1706, DIED 1790]

In the year 1716, or about that period, a boy used to be seen in the streets of Boston who was known among his schoolfellows and playmates by the name of Ben Franklin. Ben was born in 1706; so that he was now about ten years old. His father, who had come over from England, was a soap-boiler and tallow-chandler, and resided in Milk Street, not far from the Old South Church.

Ben was a bright boy at his book, and even a brighter one when at play with his comrades. He had some remarkable qualities which always seemed to give him the lead, whether at sport or in more serious matters. I might tell you a number of amusing anecdotes about him. You are acquainted, I suppose, with his famous story of the WHISTLE, and how he bought it, with a whole pocketful of coppers and afterwards repented of his bargain. But Ben had grown a great boy since those days, and had gained wisdom by experience; for it was one of his peculiarities, that no incident ever happened to him without teaching him some valuable lesson. Thus he generally profited more by his misfortunes than many people do by the most favorable events that could befall them.

Ben's face was already pretty well known to the inhabitants of Boston. The selectmen and other people of note often used to visit his father, for the sake of talking about the affairs of the town or province. Mr. Franklin was considered a person of great wisdom and integrity, and was respected by all who knew him, although he supported his family by the humble trade of boiling soap and making tallow candles.

While his father and the visitors were holding deep consultations about public affairs, little Ben would sit on his stool in a corner, listening with the greatest interest, as if he understood every word. Indeed, his features were so full of intelligence that there could be but little doubt, not only that he understood what was said, but that he could have expressed some very sagacious opinions out of his own mind. But in those days boys were expected to be silent in the presence of their elders. However, Ben Franklin was looked upon as a very promising lad, who would talk and act wisely by and by.

"Neighbor Franklin," his father's friends would sometanes say, "you ought to send this boy to college and make a minister of him."

"I have often thought of it," his father would reply; "and my brother Benjamin promises to give him a great many volumes of manuscript sermons, in case he should he educated for the church. But I have a large family to support, and cannot afford the expense."

In fact, Mr. Franklin found it so difficult to provide bread for his family, that, when the boy was ten years old, it became necessary to take him from school. Ben was then employed in cutting candle-wicks into equal lengths and filling the moulds with tallow; and many families in Boston spent their evenings by the light of the candles which he had helped to make. Thus, you see, in his early days, as well as in his manhood, his labors contributed to throw light upon dark matters.

Busy as his life now was, Ben still found time to keep company with his former schoolfellows. He and the other boys were very fond of fishing, and spent many of their leisure hours on the margin of the mill-pond, catching flounders, perch, eels, and tomcod, which came up thither with the tide. The place where they fished is now, probably, covered with stone pavements and brick buildings, and thronged with people and with vehicles of all kinds. But at that period it was a marshy spot on the outskirts of the town, where gulls flitted and screamed overhead and salt-meadow grass grew under foot.

On the edge of the water there was a deep bed of clay, in which the boys were forced to stand while they caught their fish. Here they dabbled in mud and mire like a flock of ducks.

"This is very uncomfortable," said Ben Franklin one day to his comrades, while they were standing mid-leg deep in the quagmire.

"So it is," said the other boys. "What a pity we have no better place to stand!"

If it mad not been for Ben, nothing more would have been done or said about, the matter. Butt it was not in his nature to be sensible of an inconvenience without using his best efforts to find a remedy. So, as he and his comrades were returning from the water-side, Ben suddenly threw down his string of fish with a very determined air.

"Boys," cried he, "I have thought of a scheme which will be greatly for our benefit and for the public benefit."

It was queer enough, to be sure, to hear this little chap - this rosy-checked, ten-year-old boy - talking about schemes for the public benefit! Nevertheless, his companions were ready to listen, being assured that Ben's scheme, whatever it was, would be well worth their attention. They remembered how sagaciously he had conducted all their enterprises ever since he had been old enough to wear small-clothes.

They remembered, too, his wonderful contrivance of

sailing across the mill-pond by lying flat on his back in the water and allowing himself to be drawn along by a paper kite. If Ben could do that, he might certainly do anything.

"What is your scheme, Ben? - what is it?" cried they all.

It so happened that they had now come to a spot of ground where a new house was to be built. Scattered round about lay a great many large stones which were to be used for the cellar and foundation. Ben mounted upon the highest of these stones, so that he might speak with the more authority.

"You know, lads," said he, what a plague it is to be forced to stand in the quagmire yonder, - over shoes and stockings (if we wear any) in mud and water. See! I am bedaubed to the knees of my small-clothes; and you are all in the same pickle. Unless we can find some remedy for this evil, our fishing business must be entirely given up. And, surely, this would be a terrible misfortune!"

"That it would! that it would!" said his comrades, sorrowfully.

"Now, I propose," continued Master Benjamin, "that we build a wharf, for the purpose of carrying on our fisheries. You see these stones. The workmen mean to use them for the underpinning of a house; but that would be for only one man's advantage. My plan is to take these same stones and carry them to the edge of the water and build a wharf with them. This will not only enable us to carry on the fishing business with comfort and to better advantage, but it will likewise be a great convenience to boats passing up and down the stream. Thus, instead of one man, fifty, or a hundred, or a thousand, besides ourselves, may be benefited by these stones. What say you, lads? shall we build the wharf?"

Bell's proposal was received with one of those uproarious shouts wherewith boys usually express their delight at whatever completely suits their views. Nobody thought of questioning the right and justice of building a wharf with stones that belonged to another person.

"Hurrah! hurrah!" shouted they. "Let's set about it."

It was agreed that they should all be on the spot that evening and commence their grand public enterprise by moonlight. Accordingly, at the appointed time, the whole gang of youthful laborers assembled, and eagerly began to remove the stones. They had not calculated how much toil would be requisite in this important part of their undertaking. The very first stone which they laid hold of proved so heavy that it almost seemed to be fastened to the ground. Nothing but Ben Franklin's cheerful and resolute spirit could have induced them to persevere.

Ben, as might be expected, was the soul of the enterprise. By his mechanical genius, he contrived methods to lighten the labor of transporting the stones, so that one boy, under his directions, would perform as much as half a dozen if left to themselves. Whenever their spirits flagged he had some joke ready, which seemed to renew their strength, by setting them all into a roar of laughter. And when, after an hour or two of hard work, the stones were transported to the water-side, Bell Franklin was the engineer to superintend the construction of the wharf.

The boys, like a colony of ants, performed a great deal of labor by their multitude, though the individual strength of each could have accomplished but little. Finally, just as the moon sank below the horizon, the great work was finished.

"Now, boys," cried Ben, "let's give three cheers and go home to bed. To-morrow we may catch fish at our ease."

"Hurrah! hurrah! hurrah!" shouted his comrades.

Then they all went home in such an ecstasy of delight that they could hardly get a wink of sleep.

The story was not yet finished; but George's impatience caused him to interrupt it.

"How I wish that I could have helped to build that wharf!" exclaimed he. "It must have been glorious fun. Ben Franklin forever, say I."

"It was a very pretty piece of work," said Mr. Temple. "But wait till you hear the end of the story."

"Father," inquired Edward, "whereabouts in Boston was the mill-pond on which Ben built his wharf?"

"I do not exactly know," answered Mr. Temple; "but I suppose it to have been on the northern verge of the town, in the vicinity of what are now called Merrimack and Charlestown Streets. That thronged portion of the city was once a marsh. Some of it, in fact, was covered with water."

CHAPTER VIII.

As the children had no more questions to ask, Mr. Temple proceeded to relate what consequences ensued from the building of Bell Franklin's wharf.

BENJAMIN FRANKLIN.

[CONTINUED]

In the morning, when the early sunbeams were gleaming on the steeples and roofs of the town and gilding the water that surrounded it, the masons came, rubbing their eyes, to begin their work at the foundation of the new house. But, on reaching the spot, they rubbed their eyes so much the harder. What had become of their heap of stones?

"Why, Sam," said one to another, in great perplexity, "here's been some witchcraft at work while we were asleep. The stones must have flown away through the air!"

"More likely they have been stolen!" answered Sam.

"But who on earth would think of stealing a heap of stones?" cried a third. "Could a man carry them away in his pocket?"

The master mason, who was a gruff kind of man, stood scratching his head, and said nothing at first. But, looking carefully on the ground, he discerned innumerable tracks of little feet, some with shoes and some barefoot. Following these tracks with his eye, he saw that they formed a beaten path towards the water-side.

"Ah, I see what the mischief is," said he, nodding his head. "Those little rascals, the boys, - they have stolen our stones to build a wharf with!"

The masons immediately went to examine the new structure. And to say the truth, it was well worth looking at, so neatly and with such admirable skill had it been planned and finished. The stones were put together so securely that there was no danger of their being loosened by the tide, however swiftly it might sweep along. There was a broad and safe platform to stand upon, whence the little fishermen might cast their lines into deep water and draw up fish in abundance. Indeed, it almost seemed as if Ben and his comrades might be forgiven for taking the stones, because they had done their job in such a workmanlike manner.

"The chaps that built this wharf understood their business pretty well," said one of the masons. "I should not be ashamed of such a piece of work myself."

But the master mason did not seem to enjoy the joke. He was one of those unreasonable people who care a great deal more for their own rights and privileges than for the convenience of all the rest of the world.

"Sam," said he, more gruffly than usual, "go call a constable."

So Sam called a constable, and inquiries were set on foot to discover the perpetrators of the theft. In the course of the day warrants were issued, with the signature of a justice of the peace, to take the bodies of Benamin Franklin and other evil-disposed persons who had stolen a heap of stones. If the owner of the stolen property had not been more merciful than the master mason, it might have gone hard with our friend Benjamin and his fellow-laborers. But, luckily for them, the gentleman had a respect for Ben's father, and, moreover, was amused with the spirit of the whole affair. He therefore let the culprits off pretty easily.

But, when the constables were dismissed, the poor boys had to go through another trial, and receive sentence, and suffer execution, too, from their own fathers. Many a rod, I grieve to say, was worn to the stump on that unlucky night.

As for Ben, he was less afraid of a whipping than of his father's disapprobation. Mr. Franklin, as I have mentioned before, was a sagacious man, and also an inflexibly upright one. He had read much for a person in his rank of life, and had pondered upon the ways of the world, until he had gained more wisdom than a whole library of books could have taught him. Ben had a greater reverence for his father than for any other person in the world, as well on account of his spotless integrity as of his practical sense and deep views of things.

Consequently, after being released from the clutches of the law, Ben came into his father's presence with no small perturbation of mind.

"Benjamin, come hither," began Mr. Franklin, in his

customary solemn and weighty tone.

The boy approached and stood before his father's chair, waiting reverently to hear what judgment this good man would pass upon his late offence. He felt that now the right and wrong of the whole matter would be made to appear.

"Benjamin!" said his father, "what could induce you to take property which did not belong to you?"

"Why, father," replied Ben, hanging his head at first, but then lifting eyes to Mr. Franklin's face, "if it had been merely for my own benefit, I never should have dreamed of it. But I knew that the wharf would be a public convenience. If the owner of the stones should build a house with them, nobody will enjoy any advantage except himself. Now, I made use of them in a way that was for the advantage of many persons. I thought it right to aim at doing good to the greatest number."

"My son," said Mr. Franklin, solemnly, "so far as it was in your power, you have done a greater harm to the public than to the owner of the stones."

"How can that he, father?" asked Ben.

"Because," answered his father, "in building your wharf with stolen materials, you have committed a moral wrong. There is no more terrible mistake than to violate what is eternally right for the sake of a seeming expediency. Those who act upon such a principle do the utmost in their power to destroy all that is good in the world."

"Heaven forbid!" said Benjamin.

"No act," continued Mr. Franklin, "can possibly be for the benefit of the public generally which involves injustice to any individual. It would be easy to prove this by examples. But, indeed, can we suppose that our allwise and just Creator would have so ordered the affairs of the world that a wrong act should be the true method of attaining a right end? It is impious to think so. And I do verily believe, Benjamin, that almost all the public and private misery of mankind arises from a neglect of this great truth, - that evil can produce only evil, - that good ends must be wrought out by good means."

"I will never forget it again," said Benjamin, bowing his head.

"Remember," concluded his father, "that, whenever we vary from the highest rule of right, just so far we do an injury to the world. It may seem otherwise for the moment; but, both in time and in eternity, it will he found so."

To the close of his life Ben Franklin never forgot this conversation with his father; and we have reason to suppose that, in most of his public and private career, he endeavored to act upon the principles which that good and wise man had then taught him.

After the great event of building the wharf, Ben continued to cut wick-yarn and fill candle-moulds for about two years. But, as he had no love for that occupation, his father often took him to see various artisans at their work, in order to discover what trade he would prefer. Thus Ben learned the use of a great many tools, the knowledge of which afterwards proved very useful to him. But he seemed much inclined to go to sea. In order to keep him at home, and likewise to gratify his taste for letters, the lad was bound apprentice to his elder brother, who had lately set up a printing-office in Boston.

Here he had many opportunities of reading new books and of hearing instructive conversation. He exercised himself so successfully in writing compositions, that, when no more than thirteen or fourteen years old, he became a contributor to his brother's newspaper. Ben was also a versifier, if not a poet. He made two doleful ballads, - one about the shipwreck of Captain Worthilake; and the other about the pirate Black Beard, who, not long before, infested the American seas.

When Ben's verses were printed, his brother sent him to sell them to the townspeople wet from the press. "Buy my ballads!" shouted Benjamin, as he trudged through the streets with a basketful on his arm. "Who'll buy a ballad about Black Beard? A penny apiece! a penny apiece! Who'll buy my ballads?"

If one of those roughly composed and rudely printed ballads could be discovered now, it would be worth more than its weight in gold.

In this way our friend Benjamin spent his boyhood and youth, until, on account of some disagreement with his brother, he left his native town and went to Philadelphia. He landed in the latter city, a homeless and hungry young man, and bought three-pence worth of bread to satisfy his appetite. Not knowing where else to go, he entered a Quaker meeting-house, sat down, and fell fast asleep. He has not told us whether his slumbers were visited by any dreams. But it would have been a strange dream, indeed, and an incredible one, that should have foretold how great a man he was destined to become, and how much he would be honored in that very city where he was now friendless and unknown.

So here we finish our story of the childhood of Benjamin Franklin. One of these days, if you would know what he was in his manhood, you must read his own works and the history of American independence.

"Do let us hear a little more of him!" said Edward; not that I admire him so much as many other characters; but he interests me, because he was a Yankee boy."

"My dear son," replied Mr. Temple, "it would require a whole volume of talk to tell you all that is worth knowing about Benjamin Franklin. There is a very pretty anecdote of his flying a kite in the midst of a thunder-storm, and thus drawing down the lightning from the clouds and proving that it was the same thing as electricity. His whole life would be an interesting story, if we had time to tell it."

"But, pray, dear father, tell us what made him so famous," said George. "I have seen his portrait a great many tines. There is a wooden bust of him in one of our streets; and marble ones, I suppose, in some other places. And towns, and ships of war, and steamboats, and banks, and academies, and children are often named after Franklin. Why should he have grown so very famous?"

"Your question is a reasonable one, George," answered his father. "I doubt whether Franklin's philosophical discoveries, important as they were, or even his vast political services, would have given him all the fame which he acquired. It appears to me that Poor Richard's Almanac did more than anything else towards making him familiarly known to the public. As the writer of those proverbs which Poor Richard was supposed to utter, Franklin became the counsellor and household friend of almost every family in America. Thus it was the humblest of all his labors that has done the most for his fame."

"I have read some of those proverbs," remarked Edward; "but I do not like them. They are all about getting money or saving it."

"Well," said his father, "they were suited to the condition of the country; and their effect, upon the whole, has doubtless been good, although they teach men but a very small portion of their duties."

CHAPTER IX.

Hitherto Mr. Temple's narratives had all been about boys and men. But, the next evening, he bethought himself that the quiet little Emily would perhaps be glad to hear the story of a child of her own sex. He therefore resolved to narrate the youthful adventures of Christina, of Sweden, who began to be a queen at the age of no more than six years. If we have any little girls among our readers, they must not suppose that Christina is set before them as a pattern of what they ought to be. On the contrary, the tale of her life is chiefly profitable as showing the evil effects of a wrong education, which caused this daughter of a king to be both useless and unhappy. Here follows the story.

QUEEN CHRISTINA.

[BORN 1626 DIED 1689]

In the royal palace at Stockholm, the capital city of Sweden, there was horn, in 1626, a little princess. The king, her father; gave her the name of Christina, in memory of a Swedish girl with whom he had been in love. His own name was Gustavus Adolphus; and he was also called the Lion of the North, because he had gained greater fame in war than any other prince or general then alive.

With this valiant king for their commander, the Swedes had made themselves terrible to the Emperor of Germany and to the king of France, and were looked upon as the chief defence of the Protestant religion.

The little Christina was by no means a beautiful child. To confess the truth, she was remarkably plain. The queen, her mother, did not love her so much as she ought; partly, perhaps, on account of Christina's want of beauty, and also because both the king and queen had wished for a son, who might have gained as great renown in battle as his father had.

The king, however, soon became exceedingly fond of the infant princess. When Christina was very young she was taken violently sick. Gustavus Adolphus, who was several hundred miles from Stockholm, travelled night and day, and never rested until he held the poor child in his arms. On her recovery he made a solemn festival, in order to show his joy to the people of Sweden and express his gratitude to Heaven. After this event he took his daughter with him in all the journeys which he made throughout his kingdom.

Christina soon proved herself a bold and sturdy little girl. When she was two years old, the king and herself, in the course of a journey, came to the strong fortress of Colmar. On the battlements were soldiers clad in steel armor, which glittered in the sunshine. There were likewise great cannons, pointing their black months at Gustavus and little Christina, and ready to belch out their smoke and thunder; for, whenever a king enters a fortress, it is customary to receive him with a royal salute of artillery.

But the captain of the fortress met Gustavus and his

daughter as they were about to enter the gateway.

"May it please your Majesty," said he, taking off his steel cap and bowing profoundly, "I fear that, if we receive you with a salute of cannon, the little princess will be frightened almost to death."

Gustavus looked earnestly at his daughter, and was indeed apprehensive that the thunder of so many cannon might perhaps throw her into convulsions. He had almost a mind to tell the captain to let them enter the fortress quietly, as common people might have done, without all this head-splitting racket. But no; this would not do.

"Let them fire," said he, waving his hand. "Christina is a soldier's daughter, and must learn to bear the noise of cannon."

So the captain uttered the word of command, and immediately there was a terrible peal of thunder from the cannon, and such a gush of smoke that it enveloped the whole fortress in its volumes. But, amid all the din and confusion, Christina was seen clapping her little hands and laughing in an ecstasy of delight. Probably nothing ever pleased her father so much as to see that his daughter promised to be fearless as himself. He determined to educate her exactly as if she had been a boy, and to teach her all the knowledge needful to the ruler of a kingdom and the commander of an army.

But Gustavus should have remembered that Providence had created her to be a woman, and that it was not for him to make a man of her.

However, the king derived great happiness from his

beloved Christina. It must have been a pleasant sight to see the powerful monarch of Sweden playing in some magnificent hall of the palace with his merry little girl. Then he forgot that the weight of a kingdom rested upon his shoulders. He forgot that the wise Chancellor Oxenstiern was waiting to consult with him how to render Sweden the greatest nation of Europe. He forgot that the Emperor of Germany and the King of France were plotting together how they might pull him down from his throne.

Yes; Gustavus forgot all the perils, and cares, and pompous irksomeness of a royal life; and was as happy, while playing with his child, as the humblest peasant in the realm of Sweden. How gayly did they dance along the marble floor of the palace, this valiant king, with his upright, martial figure, his war-worn visage, and commanding aspect, and the small, round form of Christina, with her rosy face of childish merriment! Her little fingers were clasped in her father's hand, which had held the leading staff in many famous victories. His crown and sceptre were her playthings. She could disarm Gustavus of his sword, which was so terrible to the princes of Europe.

But, alas! the king was not long permitted to enjoy Christina's society. When she was four years old Gustavus was summoned to take command of the allied armies of Germany, which were fighting against the emperor. His greatest affliction was the necessity of parting with his child; but people in such high stations have but little opportunity for domestic happiness. He called an assembly of the senators of Sweden and confided Christina to their care, saying, that each one of them must be a father to her if he himself should fall in battle.

At the moment of his departure Christina ran towards him and began to address him with a speech which somebody had taught her for the occasion. Gustavus was busied with thoughts about the affairs of the kingdom, so that be did not immediately attend to the childish voice of his little girl. Christina, who did not love to be unnoticed, immediately stopped short and pulled him by the coat.

"Father," said she, "why do not you listen to my speech?"

In a moment the king forgot everything except that, he was parting with what he loved best in all the world. He caught the child in his arms, pressed her to his bosom, and burst into tears. Yes; though he was a brave man, and though he wore a steel corselet on his breast, and though armies were waiting for him to lead them to battle, still his heart melted within him, and he wept. Christina, too, was so afflicted that her attendants began to fear that she would actually die of grief. But probably she was soon comforted; for children seldom remember their parents quite so faithfully as their parents remember them.

For two years more Christina remained in the palace at Stockholm. The queen, her mother, had accompanied Gustavus to the wars. The child, therefore, was left to the guardianship of five of the wisest men in the kingdom. But these wise men knew better how to manage the affairs of state than how to govern and educate a little girl so as to render her a good and happy woman.

When two years had passed away, tidings were brought to Stockholm which filled everybody with triumph and sorrow at the same time. The Swedes had won a glorious victory at Lutzen. But, alas! the warlike King of Sweden, the Lion of the North, the father of our little Christina, had been slain at the foot of a great stone, which still marks the spot of that hero's death.

Soon after this sad event, a general assembly, or congress, consisting of deputations from the nobles, the cleigy, the burghers, and the peasants of Sweden, was summoned to meet at Stockholm. It was for the purpose of declaring little Christina to be Queen of Sweden and giving her the crown and sceptre of her deceased father. Silence being proclaimed, the Chancellor Oxenstiern arose.

"We desire to know," said he, "whether the people of Sweden will take the daughter of our dead king, Gustavus Adolphus, to be their queen."

When the chancellor had spoken, an old man, with white hair and in coarse apparel, stood up in the midst of the assembly. He was a peasant, Lars Larrson by name, and had spent most of his life in laboring on a farm.

"Who is this daughter of Gustavus?" asked the old man. "We do not know her. Let her be shown to us."

Then Christina was brought into the hall and placed before the old peasant. It was strange, no doubt, to see a child - a little girl of six years old - offered to the Swedes as their ruler instead of the brave king, her father, who had led then to victory so many times. Could her baby fingers wield a sword in war? Could her childish mind govern the nation wisely in peace?

But the Swedes do not appear to have asked themselves these questions. Old Lars Larrson took Christina up in his arms and gazed earnestly into her face.

He had known the great Gustavus well; and his heart was touched when he saw the likeness which the little girl bore to that heroic monarch.

"Yes," cried he, with the tears gushing down his furrowed cheeks; "this is truly the daughter of our Gustavus! Here is her father's brow! - here is his piercing eye! She is his very picture! This child shall be our queen!"

Then all the proud nobles of Sweden, and the reverend clergy, and the burghers, and the peasants, knelt down at the child's feet and kissed her hand.

"Long live Christina, Queen of Sweden!" shouted they.

Even after she was a woman grown Christina remembered the pleasure which she felt in seeing all of hose men at her feet and hearing them acknowledge her as their supreme ruler. Poor child! she was yet to learn that power does not insure happiness. As yet, however, she had not any real power. All the public business, it is true, was transacted in her name; but the kingdom was governed by a number of the most experienced statesmen, who were called a regency.

But it was considered necessary that the little queen, should be present at the public ceremonies, and should behave just as if she were in reality the ruler of the nation. When she was seven years of age, some ambassadors from the Czar of Muscovy came to the

Swedish court. They wore long beards, and were clad in a strange fashion, with furs and other outlandish ornaments; and as they were inhabitants of a half-civilized country, they did not behave like other people. The Chancellor Oxenstiern was afraid that the young queen would burst out a laughing at the first sight of these queer ambassadors, or else that she would be frightened by their unusual aspect.

"Why should I be frightened?" said the little queen. "And do you suppose that I have no better manners than to laugh? Only tell me how I must behave, and I will do it."

Accordingly, the Muscovite ambassadors were introduced; and Christina received them and answered their speeches with as much dignity and propriety as if sho had been a grown woman.

All this time, though Christina was now a queen, you must not suppose that she was left to act as she pleased. She had a preceptor, named John Mathias, who was a very learned man and capable of instructing her in all the branches of science. But there was nobody to teach her the delicate graces and gentle virtues of a woman. She was surrounded almost entirely by men, and had learned to despise the society of her own sex. At the age of nine years she was separated from her mother, whom the Swedes did not consider a proper person to be intrusted with the charge of her. No little girl who sits by a New England fireside has cause to envy Christina in the royal palace at Stockholm.

Yet she made great progress in her studies. She learned to read the classical authors of Greece and Rome, and became a great admirer of the heroes and poets of old times. Then, as for active exercises, she could ride on horseback as well as any man in her kingdom. She was fond of hunting, and could shoot at a mark with wonderful skill. But dancing was the only feminine accomplishment with which she had any acquaintance.

She was so restless in her disposition that none of her attendants were sure of a moment's quiet neither day nor night. She grew up, I am sorry to say, a very unamiable person, ill-tempered, proud, stubborn, and, in short, unfit to make those around her happy or to be happy herself. Let every little girl, who has been taught self-control and a due regard for the rights of others, thank Heaven that she has had better instruction than this poor little Queen of Sweden.

At the age of eighteen Christina was declared free to govern the kingdom by herself without the aid of a regency. At this period of her life she was a young woman of striking aspect, a good figure, and intelligent face, but very strangely dressed. She wore a short habit of gray cloth, with a man's vest over it, and a black scarf around her neck; but no jewels nor ornaments of any kind.

Yet, though Christina was so negligent of her appearance, there was something in her air and manner that proclaimed her as the ruler of a kingdom. Her eyes, it is said, had a very fierce and haughty look. Old General Wrangel, who had often caused the enemies of Sweden to tremble in battle, actually trembled himself when he encountered the eyes of the queen. But it would have been better for Christina if she could have made people love her, by means of soft and gentle looks, instead of affrighting them by such terrible glances.

And now I have told you almost all that is amusing or instructive in the childhood of Christina. Only a few more words need be said about her; for it is neither pleasant nor profitable to think of many things that she did after she grew to be a woman.

When she had worn the crown a few years, she began to consider it beneath her dignity to be called a queen, because the name implied that she belonged to the weaker sex. She therefore caused herself to be proclaimed KING; thus declaring to the world that she despised her own sex and was desirous of being ranked among men. But in the twenty-eighth year of her age Christina grew tired of royalty, and resolved to be neither a king nor a queen any longer. She took the crown from her head with her own hands, and ceased to be the ruler of Sweden. The people did not greatly regret her abdication; for she had governed them ill, and had taken much of their property to supply her extravagance.

Having thus given up her hereditary crown, Christina left Sweden and travelled over many of the countries of Europe. Everywhere she was received with great ceremony, because she was the daughter of the renowned Gustavus, and had herself been a powerful queen. Perhaps you would like to know something about her personal appearance in the latter part of time life. She is described as wearing a man's vest, a short gray petticoat, embroidered with gold and silver, and a black wig, which was thrust awry upon her head. She wore no gloves, and so seldom washed her hands that nobody could fell what had been their original color. In this strange dress, and, I suppose, without washing her hands or face, she visited the magnificent court of Louis XIV.

She died in 1689. None loved her while she lived, nor regretted her death, nor planted a single flower upon her grave. Happy are the little girls of America, who are brought up quietly and tenderly at the domestic hearth, and thus become gentle and delicate women! May none of them ever lose the loveliness of their sex by receiving such an education as that of Queen Christina!

Emily, timid, quiet, and sensitive, was the very reverse of little Christina. She seemed shocked at the idea of such a bold and masculine character as has been described in the foregoing story.

"I never could have loved her," whispered she to Mrs. Temple; and then she added, with that love of personal neatness which generally accompanies purity of heart, "It troubles me to think of her unclean hands!"

"Christina was a sad specimen of womankind indeed," said Mrs. Temple. "But it is very possible for a woman to have a strong mind, and to be fitted for the active business of life, without losing any of her natural delicacy. Perhaps some time or other Mr. Temple will tell you a story of such a woman."

It was now time for Edward to be left to repose. His brother George shook him heartily by the hand, and hoped, as he had hoped twenty times before, that tomorrow or the next day Ned's eyes would be strong enough to look the sun right in the face.

"Thank you, George," replied Edward, smiling; "but I am not half so impatient as at first. If my bodily eyesight were as good as yours, perhaps I could not see things so distinctly with my mind's eye. But now there is a light within which shows me the little Quaker artist, Ben West, and Isaac Newton with his windmill, and stubborn Sam Johnson, and stout Noll Cromwell, and shrewd Ben Franklin, and little Queen Christina, with the Swedes kneeling at her feet. It seems as if I really saw these personages face to face. So I can bear the darkness outside of me pretty well."

When Edward ceased speaking, Emily put up her mouth and kissed him as her farewell for the night.

"Ah, I forgot!" said Edward, with a sigh. "I cannot see any of your faces. What would it signify to see all the famous people in the world, if I must be blind to the faces that I love?"

"You must try to see us with your heart, my dear child," said his mother.

Edward went to bed somewhat dispirited; but, quickly falling asleep, was visited with such a pleasant dream of the sunshine and of his dearest friends that he felt the happier for it all the next day. And we hope to find him still happy when we meet again.

www.ingramcontent.com/pod-product-compliance
Lightning Source LLC
Chambersburg PA
CBHW032022040426
42448CB00006B/702